The View from Over Here

The View from Over Here

Poems by

Alba DiBello

and

Ed Ryterband

Cover design by Shay Culligan and Michael Ryterband
Cover image by Alba DiBello

ISBN: 979-8-90146-912-5
Library of Congress Control Number: 2026938481

Kelsay Books
502 South 1040 East, A-119
American Fork, Utah 84003
Kelsaybooks.com

For Patrick, still traveling Side by Side
for his unwavering support—
and to my children and their families
for all the love they've given me.

And to Ed in gratitude for this collaboration—
forged from mutual love of poetry and friendship.

For Madelyne and others close in my life
for urging me on
and to Alba for our deep
and resilient partnership.

Why Did Two Poets Create This Book Together?

This collection of poems grew from our weekly conversations over the past four years; the forging of a new friendship focused on our mutual interest in poetry and our view of the world from the perch of old age. We found ourselves looking back and looking forward but mostly considering the present and our place in it as aging poets. We both felt the urge to share our different observations about the world. The threads were similar our voices different. We decided to try a collaboration. Hence this book.

Acknowledgments

To the places where we've published or read our work: Thank you to the editors and staff where our poems have appeared.

New Verse News
Paterson Literary Review
Two River Times
US1 Worksheets

To the venues that have provided us the opportunity to do Readings.

The Atrium in Red Bank
Brookdale Community College
The Enclave in Shrewsbury
The New Brunswick Public Library
The Oceanside Library
Parkside Lounge in NYC
The Red Bank Library

To the reviewers (blurbers) of this volume who gave us their time, attention and thoughts:

Rick Benjamin, former Poet Laureate of Rhode Island, author of *Passing Love; Some Bodies in the Grief Bed*
Maria Mazziotti, Gillan Editor of *Patterson Literary Review*; recipient of the 2008 American Book Award for *All That Lies Between Us*
Susanna Rich, producer of Wild Nights Productions, LLC; professor emerita at Kean University; and author of *Surfing for Jesus; Shout*

To the many gifted poets who have workshopped these poems:

Delaware Valley Poets
Mature Writers Workshop Paterson Poetry Center
Nan Bryan Creative Writing Workshop
US1 Poets

Contents

BODY PARTS

THE END GAME

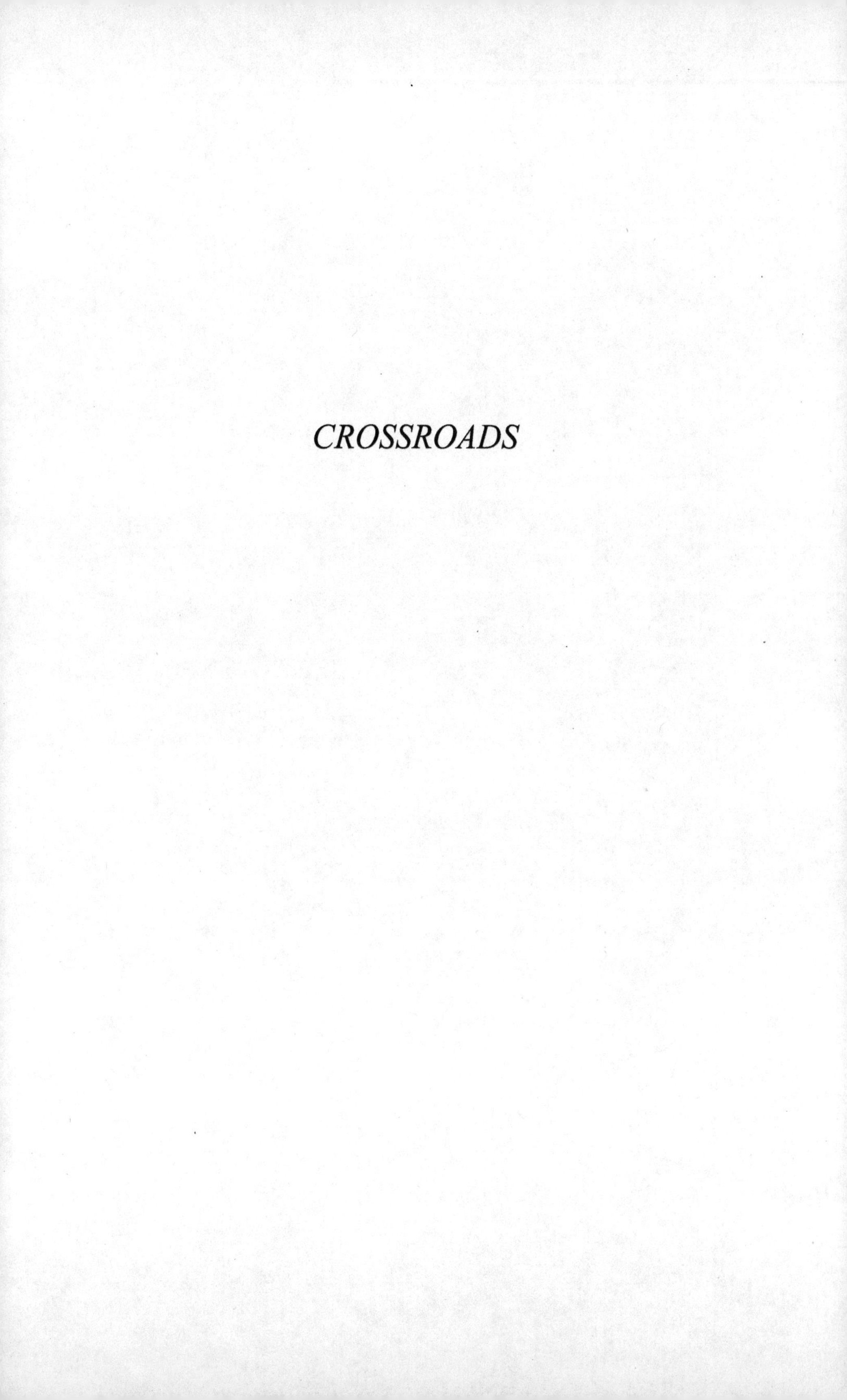

CROSSROADS

The Retirement Conversation

Retire?
Why would I? At this age?
So young?

Why wouldn't you?
I love what I do.
At the top of my game.

Do you love it more than life?
It is my life.
Maybe there's another life?
I'm in no hurry;
there's time.

Consider this.
Starting now it will take two years
to pack the boxes,
another two years to unpack them
into new places
to find out who else you may be.

Not sure I want to be someone else.
Much less, really old.
Not doing what I love.

Living Long—extra time bonus
gives you space for the great
gift of reinvention,
comes wrapped in ambiguities,
unknowns and maybe adventure.

A mixed bag to be sure.
How can you not
open that gift,
poke around the possibilities,
find out who else you might be?

Ed

Still Working After All These Years

I'm getting old,
at least by the numbers,
but
I keep the stalker at bay.

An acquaintance asks
as if it's the thing to do.
What will you do when you retire?
Waits to hear my cheerful blueprint.

What's the hurry?
I love my work, my colleagues.
I'm told I am "the best."
I get reassuring compensation.

I'm in good health,
says my growing team of doctors.
Spend indolent days beside the sea?
Play Twitchy Pickleball, Geezer Golf?

I want another dose of work.
I know how to win
run the maze
get the cheese at tunnel's end.

But now
my latest cheese hunt done,
I sit behind my desk.
A confession insists.

I could be my oldest colleagues' father.
I touch my spotted face.
I concede my slower gait.
They must see these things

whisper to each other.
They think I'm hanging on.
I can't go on
wondering, embarrassed.

I declare *Enough.*
I'll give up all the deadlines and the deference.
I know there'll be gold watches, speeches.
At home the mornings after . . .

Bill of Sale

A quality of loss affecting our content
As trade had suddenly encroached
Upon a Sacrament
—Emily Dickinson, "A Light Exists in Spring"

It is time to execute
The Bill of Sale.
My special place
My vision, my creation,
Now up for sale,
Sold.

I knew this moment had to come—
I called upon the Universe
To show the exit.
The pain was a surprise.
A sacred space
I thought it was
And hold it still.

The Bill of Sale says NO.
It says over.
It says time to go.
It had to be,
The Bill of Sale made it so.

I cannot weep for the loss.
A contract made,
Gain passed hands.
Time finally to be free.
The pain was a surprise—
The Bill of Sale slapped my cheek.

Trade had suddenly encroached upon a sacrament.

Cleaning My Files

I shredded so many Words today,
Watched them reduced to
  tiny
    strips
      of no meaning
Newsletters/articles/reports/all
Filled with Words,
My Words,
Now packing material,
Stuffing for a puppet.

My words given freely,
To guide/to provoke/
To support/to amuse—
Anyone's to read or discard.

Some readers now dead
Perhaps/but my Words once read,
Remembered, maybe even said again,
By someone new/
Had a life for a time.

So many Words
  shredded
    and gone/
      as are those
Who read them and applauded.

The Physics of Time and Me

I've kept a secret wish.
Time would pass me by.
At least slow down for me.
I'd be a miracle.

Not impossible.
No big aches or pains, no paunch.
Yes, some creaking in my joints,
a tickle from that tuft of nose hair.

Last week a young man asked
after he had called me *sir,*
Are you really in your eighties?
I smiled. *Thanks for your surprise.*

I feel like I am in my 40s.
But, there really is that nose hair.
More bad news:
I still can count.

Moving Boxes

We used to get them
From the liquor store,
Cartons to sort and pack stuff in.
How much nicer you can buy them now.
All uniform and new in white or tan with lines
Where you can write:
Contents/Date/Where to Store,
A new home for you and your files

To help us sort—
Who we were
Who we are
Who we will be,
What we need now
What we might need
What we do not need.

So much sorting
Before you can launch a new chapter.
Marie Kondo has taught us
To discard is holier than to preserve.

No one wants to look at your past
Except you.

And you just want to take a quick peak
Now and then
To remind you who you were.

Mary Oliver invites us to imagine
A world without us in it.[1]

It takes courage to
Imagine yourself
Into a new world
Where no one knows you
Or who you were.

---

[1] *After Mary Oliver's "October"*

Notes from Aboveground

Where we live now

A community for over 55
which means one of us
is at least 55 years old.
That's the rule.
They have many rules here.

I have been told
that's what makes it attractive,
conformity to rules,
an integrated aesthetic
not quite all
exactly alike,
just similar
like birds
of a feather.

I am not sure I like living
in a flock
of like-colored birds or in
a community of
like-colored
front doors.

Ed

August Surrender

A cloudless twilight
full of expectations

lawns dried and patchy
shoulder curvy streets

a soft breeze
offers up forgetfulness.

The sun finished
the sky dimmer

trees whisper
lingering goodbyes.

No neighbors out
just us two

refreshed
inside the sunset

looking around and at each other
sharing our hopes in this new home

our new village very planned,
55 and over.

All our days are numbered.
Smaller numbers

challenge us to capture peace.
Nestle in this twilight,

let the evening be enough.

A Rock in My Garden

There is a rock in my garden
hauled home in my beach bag
from a Maine vacation
a few years back
placed in the sun on
a small white table
next to my chair
in my garden patio.

It asks nothing of me.
I ask nothing of it.
Its odd shape fits my hand.
Warmed by the sun, it
offers me warmth
for free.

No commitments.
No dime in the meter.
No card to swipe.

Butterfly Time

A Monarch
impossible orange and black
wings around my garden

notices this stranger
skitters off
alights upon a fencepost

watches me.
We both stay still
a Butterfly hour

until she lifts up
into her sultry universe
darts here

and there
across the dewy air
alive with Dahlia invitations.

Wings flicker quicker
threadlike legs touch down
into a scarlet host

then another
gathering for her
Butterfly season . . .

Our moments merge
and separate until
she flutters toward me

floats around my eyes
then flies off
into her remaining time.

Ed

Nostalgias

I have this cherished album of my younger days
I keep inside my temporal lobes
where I retrieve my stories when I need them
summon my town crier
to proclaim some reassuring recollection.

I refresh these yarns about my special times
plump them into more alluring trappings
new and bright gift wrappings
wishes for affections dressed as
offerings to sometimes perfect strangers

but most of all to you
to embrace me yet again.
I hope you will indulge me.
I'm aging with what grace I can.
In return I offer some restraint,

won't allow my efforts to intrude too much
take us too much from our other pleasures
like the villains and the heroes
we watch sitting close and warm
inside our high-def evenings.

Thinking of Max and You

after Where the Wild Things Are *by Maurice Sendak*

I see the little boy Max in his wolf suit
In my favorite book for children and adults
Who remember being children.

"We love you so!" his fans shout.
I love him so, as well,
To keep close
All dressed in my own wolf suit.

Max was wild in his play,
Wilder in his imagination.
A powerful conjurer of monsters
Who he alone could command,
Captain of his own little boat.

He knew when to come back,
And when he did,
His supper was still warm.

Just like my safe harbor
Your love still warm
Even after I have been away
On my travels, real or conjured.

Our Seasons

Cocooned inside forever nights
we put off waking,
give in at last to fragile dawn light
inching onto icy blue horizons.

Beyond the oak front door
we just had painted red,
April rains bathe
our budding oaks and maples.

Day heat vapors rise up
into leaf-filled branches.
Twilights linger, invite us to a sky top
dusted end to end with stars.

Gilt and ochre-leaf clouds
shimmer through the shorter days,
drift down and settle
on our newly frosted, acorn-dotted lawn.

NEW SELFIES

Set Fire to the Rain

After Adele

The title of a song I fall for
sung by a woman,
her so alluring voice

so very pop
so not hip or cool,
still worms inside my ears.

I hum along, mouth the words.
Start to dance around my den.
Rev up my dated moves.

My desire, strong enough,
overcomes my wall of doubts
over my remaining sleekness.

Nostalgia—Only Allowed in Small Doses in the New Life

Looking at an image[2]

The brilliant blue of the sky—backdrop
Etched by a patchwork of
Glass and steel
Shimmering in the sunlight.

Cathedrals for new devotions—
Arrogant yet sometimes inspired
Human work.
Not majestic mountain peaks

Formed by nature
Yet aspiring,
Reaching,
Stretching skyward,

Anchored in a garden of concrete
Held by steadfast sidewalks
Unforgiving, hard.
Sometimes when I walked there

---

[2] *A photo of skyscrapers the author took in NYC.*

On those long streets I was surprised
By flowers growing in boxes
Or a strangers' smile.
I miss it.

Being there,
Even as I walk soft green
Garden paths now
Strewn with wildflowers,
Anointed with quiet.

All-Night Diner Mood

I look over at the *Tropicana,*
a city diner hooker-
neon and nightglow,
her metal skin
tight and sparkly.

Inside, a long gray counter
girdled by a dozen bolted stools
topped in lipstick crimson Naugahyde,
some occupied by night folks,
their backs turned to mostly empty booths.

Near the front door
fat old cakes pose shameless,
display case fluorescence
showing off their frostings
cracked with age.

Through the windows
passersby like me can see
diner people pick at meatloaf
scoop up eggs,
home fries awash in ketchup.

The night folks leave her
sated and unmoved.

Storm Clouds

We take notice
when thunderheads roll in,
sky darkens in midday,
greyness engulfs.

Loud rolls, sharp cracks,
as if we are breaking
in half.
Rain comes heavy.

We watch flooding drain spouts
swelling streets.
Sewers cry out *enough*
unable to be in charge.

A slight tremor in the heart
remains
when dark sky
recedes slowly.

Rain Witness

I am safe and still
inside the discreet beauty of this moment
wrap myself inside the autumn rain
resign the past
pay nothing to the future

choose to be just here,
witness on our back porch
the forest fifty-feet away,
a billion rain drops
announced upon a million leaves.

I flow into
see-through sheets of rain
cascade with them
down the trees

greet sporadic chirps and squawks
from unseen birds
turn back,
rejoin the present moment's rainfall.

The scene unfolds
one minute,
then the next.

I sit here
on our back porch,
a witness.

I look
listen

disappear.

Ode to Winter

I prefer the cold,
sharp edges of winter.
Intersecting planes bring clarity,
defining lines etched against sky.
White, black, tonal grey ease the eye alert—
air bites, cold embraces wake the mind.

A quiet time
of seeking shelter,
of going inside and opening doors.
Outside
short-lived, brilliant sun,
concedes to
long velvet night's blackness,
enfolding all in a dark caress.

Crystal stars are there
if I need to look up.

Reflections on a Winter Evening

Some Bad News

Canada geese, a flying V
across dusk indigo,
syncopated honks,
cascade down onto our elders' enclave.

Pinched with goose envy
I argue with my landlocked state.
The winter cold unwelcome
insists on my attention.

Nothing on the hi-def TV
to distract me
from my labors
inside frosted windows.

Night air reminders poke me.
Even after gin
no tonic transports me
to reassuring versions of hereafter.

Some Good News

Morning comes, I do concede
I am still here.
The slowly warming sun
moves handsomely across the yard

I own
because I toiled many years
and the bank said
I had what it takes to pay them back

because Mom and Daddy pleasured
one hapless end of day,
or maybe they had planned it;
no matter, my genes and I emerged

and won enough so even I have
learned to stop,
watch the late-day sunlight
follow cumulus tourists
lollygagging in the sky.

Progeny

I have a friend who
wishes to live long
enough to see his sons
as old men.
What would they look like? In their seventies?
How will they be living their lives?

I wish to see my daughters and
my grandchildren as they were.
Beautiful, swirling atoms of cosmic perfection
dropped into our lives
with open faces and piercing eyes
lighting up our dark hallways.
Blue, green, darkest brown and lightest hazel—I see
them all before me. Those eyes a jeweled garden—
a ballet of lights still dancing—
in my reverie I see them all.
Curly-haired, straight-haired, redheaded, brunette,
mischievous, serious.
So much for me to feast on as I age.
Old reels in my mind animated, all there—
running away, dressing up, cooking polenta, cracking eggs,
dancing with us. Fierce pirate and little wise one—
my memories hold them fast.

Small treasures they remain for me
unchanging in their glittering memory frames.
No need to look ahead.

Ed

Off to College

I see you standing close
curly-haired, lean and fatless.
We don't look each other in the eye.

Every picture
conjures up a vapor trail
leading back to where I've sealed you.

Steering your stroller
humming to you
in an early morning's empty streets

sitting on your bed
your eyes sweet and endless
begging for a story

scary, just enough,
a tale of pirates, Inca treasures,
hermit's ghosts.

I feel a swallow
inside jaws clenched tight,
tin whistling in my ears.

I watch the floor
eyelids squinting
like staring at the sunlight.

A long inhale rescues me.
The sob I wrestle with recedes.
Sorrows mix with benedictions for your future.

Tonight we talked about you,
the prides and wishes
we lavished on you.

Your mom
her lips squeezed out
she tried to stop . . .

I want him to come back.
I'll put him on the carpet
and just stare at him.

You're gone
except in noiseless flashes,
attic memories.

Covid Definitions, 2022

Octogenarian

How odd to have been shuffled into a new cohort
now when you would have thought
they knew who we were.
Old at Risk we are now as they refine

Covid definitions.
I am now a data point.
Dispensable—if necessary to do so.
Octogenarian, once a powerful label,

Screaming loudly, *we made it this far!*
Now redefined to a quieter
Old at Risk
starting at 75 years old.

Important data point to consider.
More of the *Old at Risk* cohort will die
than the other cohorts.
We all knew of course

we would die someday
but not to be assigned as markers on a curve,
die as data points on Covid graphs.
We rather hoped for something more personal.

Having It Out with Old Age

After Donald Hall's "Essays After 80"

I am 84.
I ignore it unless
I want to stand on one leg,
run, or throw a baseball.

I've heard all the doctors
. . . bone on bone, arthritis happens at your age.
Any falls lately? Hydrating enough? Sleeping well?
No! Maybe! Yes!

I still think respectably.
Can name all the Presidents since FDR,
solve 97% of Wordle puzzles.
Rated *Genius* in Spelling Bee sometimes.

I do forget my neighbor's name.
I rarely see him.
But he's nice enough.
I'll wish him well when I remember.

Nearby me sit nice people.
We call each other friends.
They reach out
to help me

get up from our restaurant table.
I don’t fight them off
notice their sympathetic smiles
say *thanks* cheerfully.

They do not know
the mystery
getting beyond 80
vertical.

Remember Young Love

Up the meadow slope,
a long-abandoned pasture,
two new lovers

waded through the knee-high grasses
bare legs rubbed against the slender stalks
sandaled feet undeterred by rocks
hidden in the cloak of summer blooms.
Yellow, velvet-centered daisies
teeming Queen Anne's laces
waited to be touched.
Humming bees, cicadas hissing
all the meadow's breathing
lured the lovers on
outside of time.

They reached the hilltop;
behind them lay the meadow
the hazy shapes of far-off places;

in front of them, the pond
ripples, breeze awakened,
a hundred tadpoles scattered
out among a dancing corps of water bugs.

They listened to the wind slow down
the water at their feet now still.

Her face was framed within the pond's reflection;
his shoulder touched, leaned on her
a look across the pond
a listen to the breathing of the meadow
a kiss.

Alba

My Trip to France

A solo trip
husband left behind
an army of caregivers
replace me.
An escape
an adventure/a challenge
going solo at eighty-three
to meet a friend
share an apartment
four strangers in Paris.
So many unknowns,
my cocooned comfort zone exposed.
At eighty-three I could do this,
would do this,
did this . . .
Paris, Provence, art, beauty, conversation, wine, and food

walking hand in hand
with sadness and memories of another time.
Driving crazy in our tiny VW
we pretend was a Ferrari convertible
sunroof fully open waving my underwear to dry—
surfacing memories engulf me.
I grasp at staying in the present.

I am doing this.
I did this, alone.
Never the same as then,
old places without you,
now new for me alone.
Just me
solo.

I did this without you.
Never without you.

Plastic Futures

After "To Be Human Is to Contain Plastic,"
The New York Times

I read today
we are our garbage,
we are becoming what we are discarding.

What a curious loop.

Our bodies are absorbing all those microscopic
bits of plastic we humans have created.
Our bodies are now creating
new bodies
of plastic.

Ideas have a harder time than plastics
getting absorbed.
We may in time become plastic replicas
of our former selves
impermeable to human thought

no room for ideas to root—all plastic,
we will become shiny, bright baubles
like *Bakelite Jewelry.*

Ed

Resolutions New Year's Day, 2025

Take time beside the morning window.
Watch hawks float along the treetops.
Slowly sip my coffee without sugar.

Reread Baldwin, Camus, Ram Dass.
Highlight ideas I should remember.
Attend that Ted Talk *On Apologizing.*

Visit Wikipedia.
Explore Vermeer, Glaciers, Galaxies.
Curate my playlists: Handel, Streisand, Standup Comics.

Make healthy choices.
7,000 steps, 3 times almost every week.
Eat more fruit and fiber.

Watch a TV movie M says might be good.
Rub her feet even when she dozes.
Savor her painting of the crimson dahlia.

Play iPhone solitaire to help me sleep.
Don't worry over bathroom wake-up calls.
Sleep or lie in quiet 8 hours, maybe more.

Choose to be an optimist;
I'll live through disappointment.
Cry when I'm happy, even if it's public.

Say *thanks*
when people listen
not just wait for me to finish.

I Wonder Why Old People Like to Sit in the Sun

I wonder why old people like to sit in the sun.
They do.
I've seen them
On their lawn chairs on Eastern Parkway in Brooklyn
On benches in Central Park in Manhattan
On faux Adirondack Chairs at The Mall in Shrewsbury
On the terraces of their upscale condos in Monmouth Beach.
Sun on skin
Legs spread out
Faces up.
I think it's because they relish the fact
They don't have to wear sunblock anymore.
What a gift,
Living so long that you can throw caution to the winds.

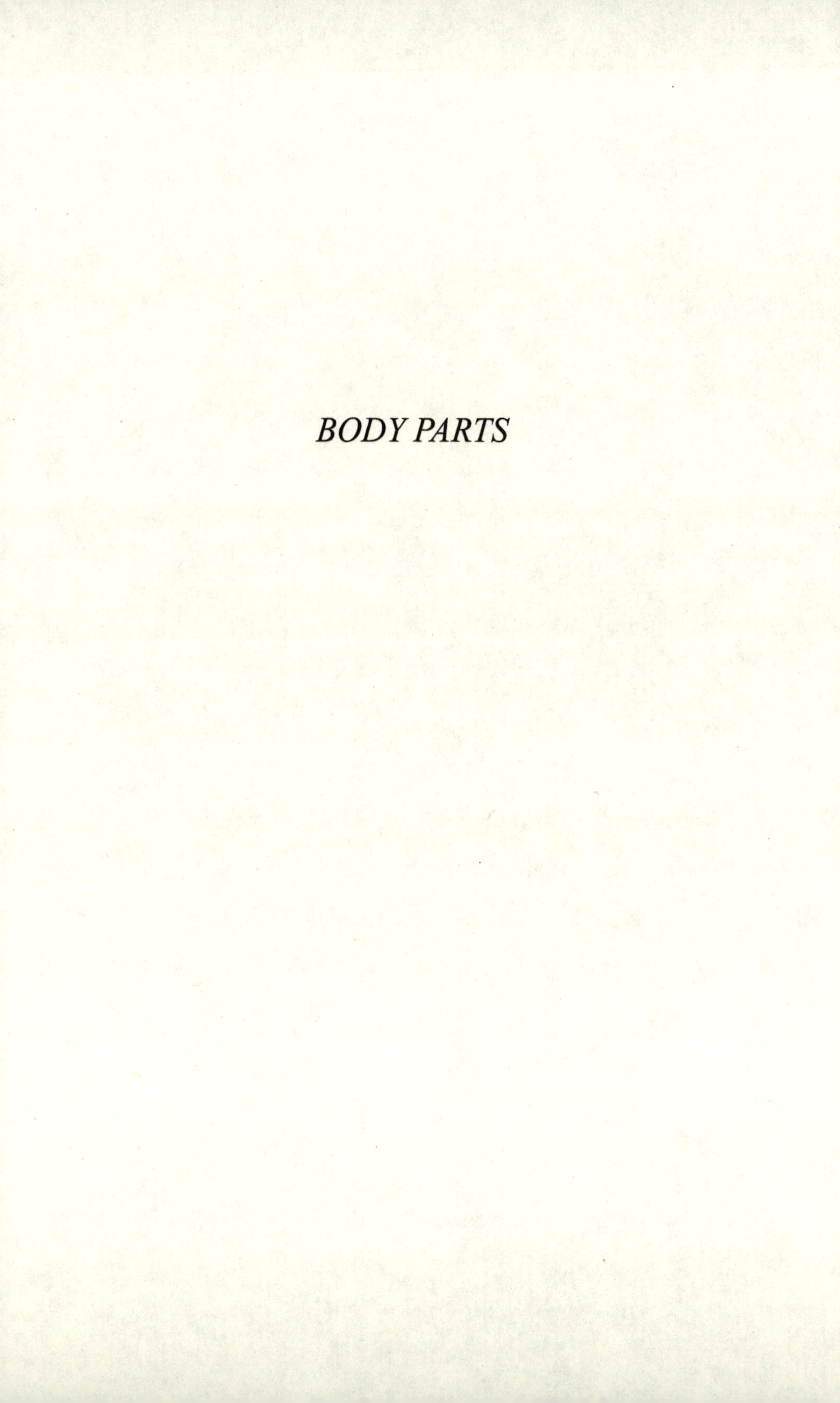

BODY PARTS

Alba

When the Body Surprises

Drooling, that's what they call it when you lust
for something or
see something that makes you salivate
in anticipation
like Pavlov's dogs.
You can taste it or feel it in your body or on your lips
like a kiss or a cupcake.
Coveted, desire-driven or nonsense drivel; all prompts
to the drool.

I am an old woman who likes to think and
see patterns in thoughts, big serious thoughts,
especially when ironing.
I am an old woman who feels her power of aged wisdom,
meditating while ironing.

I am a thinking woman
who sees a drop on the cloth right in the middle of
where she pressed her iron.
I am a wise, old woman
who sees a drop on the cloth where she ironed out
a wrinkle.
Perfectly round drop of what?
And she knows, knows suddenly,
she was drooling.
No coveted lust or desires prompted that revealing spot.
No Pavlovian kneejerk.
No drivel of thought.

I know now that I am a strong, wise woman who drools
on occasion.
I am a strong, old woman
who should remember to keep her mouth shut when
ironing.

Big Boys

They're coming home for the weekend.
40 and 34, agile, fatless.
They used to crowd the doorway.
Now I wait behind the door for them.
They're grown forever.

I've read to them in bed
seen them off to camp, to college
watched them emigrate to other lives.
I love them more than I expected.
Time is a wicked shadow.

I get the door before they ring the bell.
Come on in; put down your stuff.
How are things, Dad?
I feel like I did 30 years ago.
Together: *The problem is I still can count.*

Now I hold railings on the stairs.
Now I miss more things that people say.
Now my hand shakes when I eat my soup.
They must have noticed.

Leftovers

Why do you call us leftovers? You asked
        with a thin hint of impatience.
Because that's what we are.
        Perhaps going too far I add,
Carefully wrapped and well-kept.

Stored leftovers
waiting to be thrown out
is what I see.
Discarded bits and pieces
from a banquet
remembered on occasion.

Leftovers become unappetizing over time just like us,
I say out loud to affirm my point.

What if we put a touch on the inner thigh,
add a few squeezes of pelvic lifts and sprinkle
it all with some spicy talk might we not turn
those leftovers into a tasty dish? you ask with a sly smile.

A tasty dish fit for the king, I quip while
admiring your desire to feel and to keep living
even on the leftovers platter.

Ed

Dancing in Our Den

A song about a summer love
I find net-surfing in another idle time
penetrates my torpor
banks the coals inside
my embers catch.

The snappy tempo pushes
harmonies insist
my senior's muscles try to quicken
I should sing along
even tap my feet
maybe do some dancing in our den.

A singer who I never heard of
his sound arrangements
lift up my ole bones.
In this moment I don't care
about the world
its words and explanations.

I perk up and I rise up
allow the singer to connect
spur me on
to romp a little in our den
maybe shape a memory
I'll save and even write about.

If I choose to write to someone
it surely will be you
where I feel safe at last
to let me loose inside the music
a lot of years with you

where things went better than expected.
This tune and you
tell me tap my feet
maybe even dance with you
a little dancing in our den.

Two 40-Something Teachers in Conversation

Overheard at the gym during a workout class

A *Do old people feel pain?*

B *Probably not as much as younger people, you know, people who are out and about and feeling all kinds of sensations all the time.*

A *Really? I'm not sure about that. I have seen them wince when they prick their fingers to test their sugar levels. Of course, that's a direct hit—a direct prick.*

B *They do have numbness in their feet. Numb feet might mean not much feeling from the bottom up.*

A *How about in the head and heart?*

B *You mean like a heart attack. Or headaches?*

A *No, I mean like feelings. Emotions. Do old people hurt? Do their feelings get hurt? Do they really have feelings besides being happy to be alive? If they are happy, that is.*

B *Well—they like smile or nod off a lot, not much range there.*

A *But do you think they still hurt each other's feelings? Do friends, spouses, partners, significant others hurt their feelings?*

B *Come on now, aren't they used to it? I mean if you are in your eighties, you have probably been in the same dance for a long time; doesn't it stop hurting when your partner steps on your toe? I mean you know; you know it's coming, and your feet are numb anyway if you're old. Nothing you haven't felt before, even if you are still feeling. So why can it still hurt?*

Ed

The Looks of Love

In the beginning
was our raw, erotic clamor.
Phosphoric flashes consumed us.
In the mornings we woke hungry
for the danger and the wonder
in each other's flesh.

Then came fateful choices
giving up our blood and juices into babies,
aliens who conquered spaces we once called our own.
We reveled in their laughter and their triumphs.
The years have helped us blur the endless tending
to their cries and smells and disappointments.

Now in our evening mirror, is this older couple
who've kept on all these years,
worn smooth like stones in rivers
rounded from the flow of countless days.
We touch each other still
less frequent, more distracted.

We've traveled all these places
together, sometimes self-immersed.
Kept on showing up
because we said we would.

We laugh, we cry, we fight.
Wish aloud the other would grow different.

Somehow we repair
hold at bay the fears that linger
confess our debts
choose to still believe
there will be ways to love ahead.

He Has Another Bloody Nose

Rubbing his hands
Now filled with blood, she says,
Joking, *Out dam spot. Look Macbeth*
You have blood on your hands.
He chuckles barely/tries to smile
For her sake maybe.
As she cleans the blood she is really looking
At how unfamiliar his hands are to her now.
Misshapen fingers
Seeming to struggle out
Of their assigned positions
Wanting to make new twisted configurations.
Hands that once explored her body
Made her feel electric/gone,
Fingers new now
Unable to grasp/
Wanting to grow wildly away from each other
Come together, she silently wills them/
Come and caress/
Hold me suspended in pleasure, she orders.
They ignore her.

Ed

My Night Nurse

Her words arrive from beyond my daze.
I'll be here for you throughout the night.
My nurse, this cancer ward, us new exiles
on the first stop after surgeries
invasions unwanted that may slow or even kill a tumor
help us live some more suddenly uncertain time.

That night begins, a whirl of aches and mysteries.
She helps me walk some laps around the ward,
I.V. drip and catheter in tow.
My new life
a struggle inside my equipment
my new body cut and tied, and clean I hope.

How long to walk? Should I thank her?
She holds my arm, reveals herself.
My parents had no choice with me.
I had to be a nurse. I wanted nothing else.
These past two years made me tougher than I was at 21.
Despite her age

I bequeath her all my pain and fear
do my laps, earn my rest.
My muted whimpers yield at last to sleep.
Untold minutes on, deep inside that night,
she wakes me, sits me up in bed
a few soft words, some meds.

Then again, at dawn
she asks me *Try to sit without my help.*
I look at her, feel safe to try.
Her promise kept for me and all of us
she keeps returning to our bedsides
regardless of the losses.

In the ER with Family and Friends

Emergency Room bustle
Death—maybe soon.
I see loved ones; faces drawn,
pinched lips.
I sit up—smile—
fall over.
Bells ring—lights flash alarms—
hands all over me.
I vomit, cough, and sit up again.
Notice a new face.

You died five times in there, says the gentle Doctor.
Stranger now a savior
come to offer life again.
I don't want a foreign gizmo in my body, I state loudly.
Summoning resolve, defiant, I shout,
I can do this without a pacemaker!
Calmly, nodding slightly he says,
Your heart stops like that again, and you will be dead.
I don't believe him.

Clever, he suggests a temporary device.
It can be removed tomorrow, he says reassuringly.
I accept, and there is a night of fitful sleep
no bells or alarms
just shadows and whispers.

Elder Morning

Fewer clocks, insistent calls to hurry up
be somewhere else,
this morning unfolds without a jumpstart.

I listen to my chest fill out
strum along inside my head.
Eyelids gently lift.

I meander among unconnected musings
allow the urge to rise up
surrender to this portion of my shrinking life.

I lift myself to vertical,
creak, and laugh it off,
park it in the padding of memories,

reimagine bygone lovers
relish their pastime succulence.

Across my neatly ordered bedroom
on its proper stand
my smartish phone

comfort and umbilicus
plugs me into any world I choose.
Handel or The Beatles on the playlist for today.

My life now a Greek diner
lots of choices on the menu,
some not fresh

but choose we must.
I pick one for no reason,
nothing left to prove.

Time has come to be inside my earbuds,
a duvet of soft encounters.
I've made it to being old.

Let Us Always Wear Lipstick

For my friend Frieda after our FaceTime call

What a lift it was to see
Those red lips, dear friend

Frame your beautiful smile.
Let us always wear lipstick.

It is of our time, and we
Celebrate it as we rejoice

Lives lived well.
Fire and Ice.
Love That Red.
Cherries in the Snow.

How many can you name?
Our lips announced who we were,

And we intended to be noticed.

Pale lips came into vogue,

Along with pale and angry voices.
Then no lips and no makeup

An intentional face

For an intentional generation,
Whatever that was supposed to mean.

But you wore it anyway as did I.
Bright red and bright pink.

Bright and bold as we are now.
Let us always wear lipstick,

It is who we are
Not all we are.

Old Friend in Frankfurt

I fly across an ocean
and our fifty years
to be with you again.
We have this week.

We walk your streets and parks
hours traveled without words
among flowing streams of people
who do not notice us.

I wobble, you can see it.
I insist we should go on.
On stairs you catch your breath
complain a bit and shrug.

We are not arm-in-arm.
Rarely look at one another.
We do go side by side
inside each other.

You talk to me in my tongue.
I feel the warm within
the rumble of your low voice
looking after me.

How do you feel this morning?
Did you sleep well?
What would you like to do today?

You stop our Sunday morning walk.
What will I do when you have left?
We may not have this time again.

I stop, look into you.

In Mid-March

In mid-March
I wait for Spring-
like days
due us
after enduring cold rains
and wild winds at winter's end.

Nature gives a gold star
if you make it through—
flowers will bloom for you.
You, still here
to celebrate
another renewal.

It's easier now.
Nothing to prove,
no new hill to climb
unless you choose to.
You have made it this far.
Your reward is yourself.

There is no cruelty in April
As TS would have us believe,
not for us old people.

April is awards month,
time to collect mine—

in my nightgown
if I so choose,
or standing naked
in front of a mirror,
impressed.

44 Years and Counting

I want you very much to love me.
Who is better
my tenured partner
to nudge me to my next appointments?

You are audience and leading lady
featured in my fables
stories I bring to life
burnished conquests and rebellions.

Time pokes me with its wicked finger.
You help me hold my ground
sometimes stare it down
distract me when I need it.

Your comforts help me
embrace my soft illusions
moments when I might forget.

I'm in a life that ends without you
a time I give infrequent notice to
will surely come

foist itself upon me
like a cat upon an unsuspecting mouse.

THE END GAME

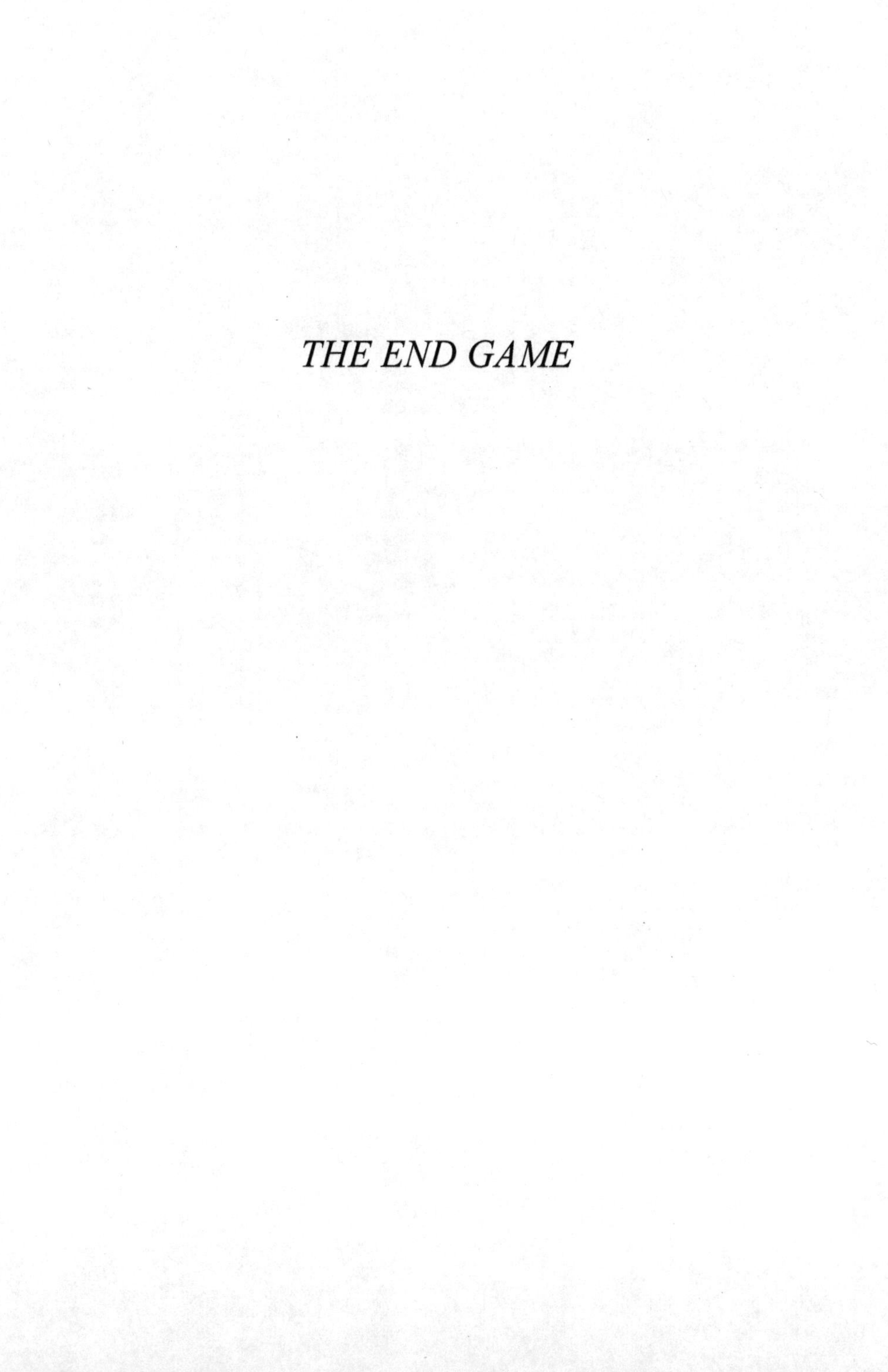

Summer End

AND what is so rare as a day in June?
Then, if ever, come perfect days.
—James Russell Lowell, "And what is so rare as a day in June?"

AND what is so delightful a gift as a late August day?
Where there is no expectation of rarity or perfection,
it is the end that captivates and invites attention.
A day of spent heat and subdued breeze beckons.
Dazzling light, sun warm and shade cool.
My willow tossing its long hair drying in the gentle wind.
Geraniums bobbing their heavy heads still wet with dew,
nodding off in a mid-morning nap.
Roses hanging on, refusing to miss the last show.
Crickets oblige, sing louder of summer nights'
fading memories.

I am seduced by this day.
I wish nothing more than to stretch on my lounge
loose and languid, ignoring my morning coffee.
It is the end of this season of undoing,
of letting go, untying knots,
unravelling constraints.

Come blow on the dandelions and scatter seeds.
Daydreaming calls and offers warm comforts.
All too soon it will end.
In the meantime, *E dolce far niente.*[3]

---

[3] *"It is sweet to do nothing," from the Italian.*

Ed

My Late-Autumn Walk

A new path curves
into this autumn wood.
My feet beget
crunching, crackling twigs
sinking into dirt and rotting leaves.

I stop, stand still
look up from my feet sounds
scan the unmarked trail
regain my breath
reassure my balance.

Up ahead, more brown, grey,
unlikely blue above
grass awaiting frost.
I see the soft hill rise
slowly, let a breath go, and
I follow it.

Getting Ready for a New Season

Leaves in blazing hues
wind gusts of fall chill
sun shifts to long, low light,
here I am with summer-white
pants in my closet,
white sandals on my shoe rack,
searching for long-sleeve shirts,
too many shorts
not ready.

Less time to
put things off
age stacks years
leaves no wiggle room
to be ready
before the final season.

Living is much more
compelling
than packing up for death,
I procrastinate
buy a big orange pumpkin
for my porch
greet the new season
in my white shorts.

Ed

The Crow, the Worm, and I

The Crow doesn't live as long as I do.
But the crow doesn't know about Famine;
there's probably something
laying around dying to be taken.

The Worm doesn't live as long as the crow.
But worms don't know about Flood;
they just take whatever comfort
inside the earth's dark protection.

I look ahead.
I look around.
I know.

Two Old Friends Sitting Outside on a Fall Afternoon

Lawn chairs Coffee Coral
our patch of light amidst shadows
we will outlast

even as we know they are getting longer
stretching ever towards us

we sit like two lizards happy to be warm
without having to warm each other.

Shadows are always longer this time of year, we say.
We move our chairs to keep them at bay.

Loved One

I found some time for you today
reached outside

my ruminations over
getting on in years.

I found you again.
Your dark and curly hair, peasant blouse,

the laughing girl
who long ago conceded

you would go your separate way
that day I claimed I needed to move on.

I sort through tattered recollections.
We were not meant to be.

I lost touch with you these many years
because I did.

Today I put aside
the pinch of my regrets

made my way
back into our better times.

I'm told you've died.
You cannot hear me now.

Necessary Rituals

Funerals, Wakes, Celebrations of Life

Old people really like to go to funerals
make a showing
despite the aches and pains
of sitting on uncomfortable chairs
suffering heavy floral scents.
They assure themselves
they are VIP witnesses.

They smile and nod at others
check cards/floral displays
dresses and guest books
stealing looks
to the back
while sitting up front
nearest casket or urn,
perusing the old photographs placed there.

Amazing, they say to each other,
So many people.
People I haven't seen in years.
Even the children that we barely saw,
they all came to the funeral.

They think to themselves,

Why don't they come to visit before
when you could maybe chat a bit?

Who They Were

Survivor Notes

I open the door to the basement
try not to hold the railing
test my old age balance
flip on the basement lights
turn toward the far corner
scan the jumble of boxes.

On top of one pile
Mom and Dad's gray suitcase
the stiff old kind, a Samsonite
with no wheels, they packed
for their retirement vacation trips
to Montreal, Puerto Rico, London.

Their initials, M&J,
stamped in crusted latches
I tug until they yield.
Mold smells rise from fabric pockets.
Slowly I unwrap the yellowed newsprint
safeguarding the framed Kodak color photos.

One by one, I hold them up.

Mom smiles, looking down,
her hands, arthritis still in hiding,
rest on that shiny blue dress
covered in pink roses
I once tried to smell.
Gone 2004.

Dad glows triumphant,
        one hand on his deep-sea rod and reel,
taller than he is;
        the other holds his trophy dolphin
caught before the War and us kids arrived.
        Gone 2006.

Brother Mel smiles at the camera,
        a red-haired cherub,
freckles cover fat and rosy cheeks.
        A Gerber Baby lookalike
slept in my bedroom.
        Gone 2020.

The toddler standing on the stoop
        of the little stucco house:
that's me, two years old,
        showing off a grapefruit
from our very own tree.
        Still Here 2025.

I visit each of them,
        linger inside memories as fond as my desires.
A sting grows inside my eyes,
        then that dry swallow.
I rewrap them, tuck them
        gently back into the suitcase.

Ed

Our Dying

Surely there will be my going black
some day not far enough away.
I might rave, maybe shit myself
in my surrender to the vampire
as it gathers to enfold me
my final slipping into darkness.

That night my father's end closed in
he left his bed and fell.
He likely cursed the god
he swore was never there.
I come to see him
lying mute, skin thin and gray
face turned up to the ceiling.
His open eyes are still
fluorescence glowing without judgment
above his hospice bed.

There is no consolation for our dying
in biblical hereafter promises
or movie heroes "passing" gracefully.
I've had a good run; time to go
see you on the other side . . .
Counterfeit concessions.

He holds my hand.
Do I hold his?
I watch myself
stare silent at the window
then at him, again at him.
He lies there, mouth and body slack.
Morphine dribbles into him.
The darkness in his open speechless mouth,
I stare at it, remember, shudder,
weep for both of us.

Up at Lou's place

For Patrick after cardiac diagnosis

We were so very young and so full
of each other
finding joy
in being together.

We would pile in the car
go up to Lou's Place
where we skated at night on the lake
in the dark near thin ice.

Knowing the dangers
we kept to the middle
ice, frozen thick,
avoided the edges.

Remember
at night you could hear
soft owl sounds, gentle snow winds
whistling in trees,
then loud CRACKS startled.

Splitting ice/spring thaw.
The earth was moving
without us.
We laughed, held each other

keeping the edges at bay
warm and emboldened
in our sleeping bag all day
discovering each other.

We could see so well on the lake at night.
Big Moon lantern and little cabin lights playing
on snow and ice so white, with edges showing a slip of blue,
I can still see those edges.

You barely knew how to skate and
held on to me, but not for long.
Once you went too close
being you and the ice gave—

your leg went in but you
grabbed at a tree branch
saved yourself
came out laughing and wet.

You liked to do that,
skate near the edges.
You loved that danger zone
as did I.

Now we are surrounded by edges.
What do we want *more* from this life.
You have a branch to grab or not;
perhaps you will just let it go.

We can't see in the dark the way we could at the lake.
The moon hides as much as it shows.
We still find each other under covers;
now you make the soft night sounds like an owl.

Watching you sleep in the afternoon,
are you skating near the edges
where I don't want to go,
not yet.

The Hand of God

The Bible's scribes proclaim,
Accept His path to virtue here.
His Kingdom surely will be there for you.
Accept our God who truly is your God.
Go our way.
There is no other.

The New Age Pundits offer,
There is no god.
Just particles.
Ahead a dirt nap in forever.
Here and Now is all there is.
Freedom's born with your embrace.

I turn away from all those voices.
Wrap myself within my old-man hopes.
You are there, behind the heavens' rhythms.
You set the world in motion.
Then left us here to be
among the cities, villages, and lonely farms,

forests, oceans, mountains, deserts,
the feel of rain and baby skin,
the smells of bacon, day-old socks . . .

Your hand designed this planet speck
so unlikely, amid countless galaxies
endless cold and empty space.

Your gift
despoiled though it is.
I take Your hand.
You are benign, indifferent.
Enough for my surrender.

Notes for You Should You Need Them

It occurs to me
watching you work out
with your therapist—getting stronger,
you may outlive me.
Should I die before you
here are a few notes should you need them.

Be sure to:

Tell them I had a great sense of humor
that wasn't always apparent to others.
Tell them I loved to make love with you;
some people won't know that.
Tell them I was never afraid.
You can tell them you taught me that.
Tell them I had passions,
and a passion to do the best I could,
almost perfect, my goal, almost always.
Tell them I loved a good fight
and good chocolates, that
I loved all the old people and children
who populated my life, and my ancestors
who gave me form and spirit.
Tell them I loved our daughters best and
their children, and their children.

And tell them that
I loved you for a lifetime,
never easy.
Tell them I have no regrets save
I only wish I had tasted more
drank more deeply from the fountain
danced longer at the fair
not worked so hard to be the best.

Then invite them all
to read a poem
sing a song
play the accordion
drink Martinis
praise the powers that be.

I had a good life, almost perfect.
Tell them they can too.
Be sure to tell them that for me.

Ed

Mother's Gone

Your hours have no song or nectar any more.
They pass like cats slipping by your screen door.
Your eyes stare fixed like hazel stones
your world shrunk to food and sleep
perhaps a word you maybe hear,
a prize for us one random day.

The doctor
so clinical and certain, said,
Nothing to be done.
She's reached beyond the golden years.

I wander back into last May.
Where I sat close by you
praised the Fichus trees around the pool
the cotton shapes drifting in the southern sky,
imagined conversation.

I guard you now in your December
against well-wishing friends and strangers.
My patter stretches out the moments.

I see a treeless plain inside your head.

I reach out to hold your hands
touch your bulging knuckles
caress the purple roundness of your veins.
You move your hand, a silent hint,
maybe one more frail connection.

You drift off silent as a cloud.

My Plan for Becoming Dead

I am 84
will plan ahead
complete the business of becoming dead
how to dispose of me
leave what's left of me
to those who may deserve it.

I will seek wise friends
old people
who have a sense of humor.
We'll imitate old elephants
gathered 'round each other
to comfort one who's dying.

Better than old elephants
people know before our dying
our turn will surely come
a final act
like a dirt nap in forever,
maybe something better.

My old people,
they still can laugh
not seduced by hope
to fabricate a certainty.
Together we will look
and laugh and dance.

Happy 90th Birthday
Time to Burn the Bones and Pass the Martinis

So Aged one
thoughts are now of tombs
urns and balloons
rising while dreams and burial songs
take center stage and
Wooly Mammoths parade.
Shadows spread
remind us of new journeys ahead.

It is time
to burn the bones.
Pass the martinis
we need to talk
of where the bones will go
the end is near
or not,
but for sure/end it is.

The last mystery revealed.
A trip without itinerary
begins with the end
soon we must
burn the bones.
Pass the martinis.

About Alba DiBello

Alba DiBello is an educator and founder of a distinguished school for young children and NJEEPRE, a professional organization for teachers. She is also a poet, as well as a long-time student of poetry.

She began exploring writing in Zoom workshops and was mentored by local poet Nan Bryan. Encouraged by Ed Ryterband, she has recently emerged into publishing her own work. Her poetry appears in *US1 Worksheets* and *Patterson Literary Review.* She has also shared her poetry at River Read Open Mic in Red Bank, NJ. *The View from Over Here* is her first published collection.

About Ed Ryterband

Ed Ryterband is a memoirist, standup comic, and psychologist as well as a poet. His poems appear in *Patterson Literary Review, Two River Times, US1 Worksheets,* and *New Verse News.* He has four collections of poetry, all from Kelsay Books: *Life On Cloud Eight* (2019); *Beyond Cloud Eight* (2020); *Rain Witness* (2022); and *Equanimity* (2025). *Rain Witness* was nominated in 2022 for The Pushcart Prize. *Who They Were,* a memoir about life under the influence of his immigrant parents, is forthcoming.

www.ingramcontent.com/pod-product-compliance
Lightning Source LLC
LaVergne TN
LVHW090614110826
845146LV00001B/389

* 9 7 9 8 9 0 1 4 6 9 1 2 5 *